DUKE KAHANAMOKU VS. THE SURFNAPPERS

a play for young people

Eric Overmyer

BROADWAY PLAY PUBLISHING INC
New York
www.broadwayplaypublishing.com
info@broadwayplaypublishing.com

First edition: June 2019
I S B N: 978-0-88145-830-5

Book design: Marie Donovan
Page make-up: Adobe InDesign
Typeface: Palatino

DUKE KAHANAMOKU VS. THE SURFNAPPERS was commissioned by Honolulu Theatre For Youth in 1993. It was then produced by Honolulu Theatre For Youth in 1994, directed by Ron Nakahara.

CHARACTERS & SETTING

Duke Kahanamoku
Truck
Judy
Big Guy
Old Lady
Mr Double Bogey
Armond
Princess Pele
Shark

(Onstage is a pedestal that has "DUKE" engraved on the base and a big old-fashioned wooden surfboard attached to its back. One of those sixteen-foot plus, two hundred pound, teak and mahogany monsters, standing upright. Hanging upstage are four large black and white photographs, big blow-ups, head shots of Duke Ellington in top hat, Duke Snyder in his Brooklyn Dodger uniform, and DUKE KAHANAMOKU, *standing next to his giant surfboard.)*

(The CAST *comes out and offers a ritual prayer, speaking the words in turn.)*

CAST: We offer this play—

CAST: With the deepest respect and humility—

CAST: As a gift of love to Hawai'i—

CAST: And as a prayer to the great and unquenchable aloha spirit—

CAST: Of Duke Kahanamoku—

CAST: A true Hawaiian hero—

CAST: An American hero—

CAST: A hero to the whole world—

(The actor playing DUKE, *wearing shorts and a vintage aloha shirt, steps up on the pedestal and becomes the Waikiki statue of Duke Kahanamoku, arms outstretched. The rest of the cast drapes leis over his arms and around his neck, as is the custom, and exits. After a moment a teen-age* BOY *and* GIRL *enter, look at the statue.)*

BOY: Hey. Check out the statue. Who's this guy?

GIRL: *(Reads)* Duke.

BOY: Duke who?

GIRL: Beats me.

(BOY and GIRL stare at the statue, stumped.)

GIRL: Cool surfboard.

BOY: Kinda gigantic, don't ya think? Kinda gargantuan. Kinda positively prehistoric.

GIRL: Kinda cool.

BOY: I mean, who could even lift that monster?

GIRL: He could, I guess. Duke.

BOY: A big I doubt it. Come on. Let's grab our boards and hit the surf.

GIRL: No surf today.

BOY: Huh?

GIRL: *(Points)* Look. No surf. Like glass—

BOY: Weird. Let's go get a shave ice.

GIRL: Okay.

(BOY runs off. GIRL lingers, looks at the statue. She sits down and concentrates on DUKE.)

GIRL: So, who are you, anyway?

(Hawaiian music comes up. The lights go wavy, dissolve. Always an exciting effect. DUKE hops off the pedestal. Looks at the GIRL.)

DUKE: I'm so glad you asked me that question.

GIRL: *(Agog)* Whoa!

(Music and wavy lights)

(DUKE flips the board over and hops on. The board is suspended a couple of feet above the stage, and he looks great as he surfs through the air. He executes a

tricky maneuver, and laughs. He looks at the audience
and waves.

DUKE: Hi. How ya doin'? Great day for surfing, isn't it?
Of course, every day's a great day for surfing. Because
surfing's like breathing. And every day's a great day
for breathing, right? You call up your friends and you
say, hey, looks like a great day for breathing, huh?
You wanna go breathe later? I know this terrific place
for breathing. The air's fantastic. You'll love it. *(He
inhales, exhales, does another tricky move on the board.)*
See? Surfing—breathing. Same thing. *(He smiles at
the audience.)* My name's Duke. Duke Kahanamoku.
You're here to listen to my story, right? Problem is,
anybody who knew me when I was alive knows I
never talked about myself. But now that I'm a statue—
well, somebody's gotta do it, if we're gonna get this
story told. So. It's up to me. No brag, just fact. They say
I come from Hawaiian royalty. Ali'i. Hey. It must be
true. Otherwise, why would they call me Duke? Right?
'Course, I got a brother named Sargeant. So he must
come from Hawaiian military. And my other brothers
are named— *(He pulls down a screen. On it is the famous
photograph of the Kahanamoku brothers on Waikiki with
their big boards.)* Bill, Sam, Louis and David. They
got kinda shortchanged on the royal names. But
they're all Waikiki beach boys like me — pretty good
swimmers, and real good surfers. I know you hate to
study history, but this is history, too. *(He pulls down
next screen: a drawing of ancient Polynesians surfing on
traditional boards. He picks up a pointer.)* The history of
surfing! And don't let anybody tell you that the history
of surfing isn't worth studying. See, surfing had just
about died out among our people. We Hawaiians
were the world's first surfers. We invented it. We
Polynesians, I should say. Of course, the best surfers
were Hawaiian, always have been, always will be,

everybody knows that. Just don't tell those guys from Samoa, eh? But the missionaries didn't approve of surfing— *(He pulls down another screen with a drawing of tight-lipped missionaries who don't know the meaning of the word "fun". Re: drawing:)* Whoo. Scary. The missionaries thought we were just goofin' around. Bein' lazy. Havin' fun. They didn't approve of havin' fun, those missionary folks. And they didn't realize that surfing's a religious experience to us Hawaiians. Surfing's spiritual. Any serious surfer'll tell you that. Anyway, the missionaries thought we should be grouchy, like them. You know. Go around like a bunch of mopey mooks. So we tried that for awhile, we tried bein' like them, but that just made us sick. And so we practically died out and disappeared, and surfing along with us. But then we started surfing again. *(He pulls down the Kahanamoku brothers screen again.)* And when we started surfing again, our culture came back, and we started breathing again. And everybody everywhere found out that surfing is like breathing. And that's a pretty big gift from Hawaii to the world. *(He sees something on the horizon.)* I don't know if you heard, but there was an earthquake off the coast of Japan this morning. Big one. Which means— *(He checks the sun.)* The Osaka Express should be coming through here any minute now. The biggest wave you ever seen! The biggest wave anybody ever seen! *(He bends his knees and gets ready.)* Here it comes! Feel it? It's coming! I'm telling you, you never seen a wave like this! This is the great-great-great Grandmama of waves. Got to be fifty feet high! That's not so big. Okay! A hundred! A hundred feet high! Big as a skyscraper! Big as the biggest building in Chicago, which is where I went to try out for the 1912 Olympics. Boy, was it cold! I got a cramp in my legs and almost didn't make the team. Hallelujah! Let's take this baby in! All the way to the beach! Park this board under the banyan tree at the Moana Hotel. Look out! Here we go!

(He catches the wave and surfs on it, cutting back and riding across, and doing all those amazing, seemingly impossible surfing things.) Yes! Hold on! Here we go! Look out! *(He rides the great-great-great Grandmama of all waves all the way into the beach, and hops off under the banyan tree at the Moana Hotel.)* Here we are! What'd I tell you? Under the banyan tree at the Moana Hotel! Hey! This is some banyan tree, huh? The great-great-great Grandmama of banyan trees! Must be a thousand years old! At least! Two thousand, maybe! Wow! That was some ride! *(He looks out at the water.)* Reminded me of the old days at Waikiki. Under the moonlight. You could catch a wave way out, and ride it in a thousand yards, all the way to the beach, smooth as silk, just glide in, park it on the sand. You could balance a glass of water on the palm of your hand, not spill a drop. No kiddingI 'Course, we used a different kind of board back then. My board weighed two hundred pounds! No kidding! Made outa solid teak and mahogany. You had to be a pretty strong guy to even pick up an old board, much less get it out in the water. That was a long time ago. Surfing's a whole different ball game now.

(Lights come up on the picture of Duke Snyder.)

DUKE: Speaking of ballgames. Another Duke. Duke Snyder. Dodger. Brooklyn Dodger. Hall of Fame. Me, I'm in the Surfing and Swimming Hall of Fame. Surfers are the best athletes in the world, let's face it. They used to be, anyway. Now surfing's different, boards are different. And even the surf at Waikiki is different. It doesn't break the way it used to. I don't know why. You couldn't get a thousand yard ride any more at Waikiki, no matter what kind of board you were using. Things just ain't what they used to be.

(Music: a few bars of Things Ain't What They Used To Be.*)*

DUKE: Which, by the way, is the name of a song written by another Duke. *Things Ain't What They Used To Be.* Duke Ellington. The greatest American composer ever! No kidding!

(Lights come up on the famous picture of Duke Ellington, looking suave in top hat and tails. DUKE *checks it out.)*

DUKE: And a very cool dude, Check him out. Anyway, my thousand yard rides at Waikiki brought surfing back. Made it popular all over the world. I was already famous. So when people saw me surfing those thousand yard rides at Waikiki, it started a world-wide craze. Which has never stopped to this very day. No brag, just fact. I was famous for winning a gold medal in the 1912 Olympics. Swimming. One hundred meters. Stockholm, Sweden. Boy, was it cold! They said it was summertime, but you couldn't prove it by me! I also won another gold medal for the one hundred meters. 1920, Belgium. Boy, was it cold there, too! Anyway, I went to one more Olympics, 1924, Paris. It was freezing. I mean, they said it was summertime, but you couldn't prove it by me. I was the oldest member of the American swim team that year—but this time I didn't win the gold. I would've, but I caught a bad cold. I won the silver. My friend Johnny Weissmuller won the gold. You know. Johnny Weismuller. Tarzan. *(He does a Tarzan yell. Grins)* Johnny was a great swimmer. A much better swimmer than an actor. But that's another story.

(Music cue: a few bars of Gabby Pahinui. DUKE *pulls down a screen with a picture of Gabby Pahinui.)*

DUKE: That's my pal. Gabby Pahinui. Beautiful music, eh? I'll tell you more about him later. I helped start the craze for Hawaiian music, too. No brag, just fact. I mean, people saw me in my aloha shirt, up on my surfboard— *(He hops up on his surfboard.)* They just naturally went crazy for everything Hawaiian. All over the world. History. *(He points the pointer at his shirt.)* I popularized the Hawaiian shirt, too. *(He models his shirt.)* Nice one, huh? You gotta walk the walk, not just talk the talk, to wear one of these babies. *(He hops back down, pulls down screen: a Hawaiian fisherman.)* So, in Hawaii, if you see somebody goin' fishin', you don't say. Hey, goin' fishin' today, eh? —'Cause the guy goin' fishin' will just pack up his stuff and go home, 'cause it's bad luck if you say it out loud, the fish hear he's comin' and they split, and he won't catch anything, so he might as well not waste his time. But surfing's not like that. The surf's not like a fish, it's always gonna be there. Except for this one time. Which is the time I wanted to tell you about. How I came to rescue surfing from a fate worse than death—and save Hawaii.

(Music)

DUKE: I'd just gotten back from Hollywood, doing a Tarzan movie with my buddy Johnny Weismuller— *(Does Tarzan yell)* And I'd just become the new sheriff of Honolulu— *(He pins a sheriff's star on his Hawaiian shirt.)* And I was on Waikiki beach, oiling my board, when these friends of mine. Truck and Judy, come running up—

(Lights change. Wavy flashback music. DUKE oils his board. His pals, JUDY and TRUCK [the BOY and the GIRL] come running on.)

TRUCK: Hey, Duke!

JUDY: Hey, Duke!

DUKE: Truck! Judy! How ya doin'?

TRUCK: Well—

JUDY: How are you. Duke?

DUKE: Happy!

TRUCK: That's good.

JUDY: How was Gollywood?

DUKE: Oh, you know. They had me playing the Tonto part, as usual.

JUDY: So you didn't get the girl.

DUKE: Not this time.

TRUCK: Maybe next time.

JUDY: Yeah, right. Not.

TRUCK: Shut up.

DUKE: Hey, it was okay. I got to meet a lot of movie stars.

TRUCK: Cool.

(JUDY *and* TRUCK *look at each other.*)

JUDY: Uh, Duke. Coin' surfin'?

DUKE: Judy— (*Indicates board*) Duh—

JUDY: Oh, yeah. Duh. Uh, Duke? You think that's bad luck?

DUKE: Bad luck?

JUDY: To ask somebody if they're goin' surfin'?

DUKE: Judy, man, surf's not like fish. Surf's always there.

(JUDY *and* TRUCK *look at each other.*)

DUKE: So. How are you guys? Happy?

TRUCK: Mostly.

DUKE: Mostly?

TRUCK: Mostly.

DUKE: Whaddya mean, mostly?

JUDY: Mostly. Except for this one bummer item.

DUKE: Which bummer item is that?

JUDY: Uh—

TRUCK: Duke. Somethin' wacky's goin' on—

DUKE: Somethin' wacky? In Waikiki? I'm shocked.

JUDY: No, Duke. We're serious. You might not be able to go surfin' today—

DUKE: Who's gonna stop me?

TRUCK: This is gonna sound kinda strange—

JUDY: There's no surf.

DUKE: Whaddya mean, no surf? There's always surf.

JUDY: Not today.

TRUCK: It's gone. Vanished.

JUDY: Like, nowhere to be found.

DUKE: What's so wacky about that? Happens, man. No big deal. Full moon or something. It'll be back tomorrow.

TRUCK: No, man. You're not listening. We mean the surf is gone.

JUDY: Outa here.

TRUCK: Vamanos. It disappeared two weeks ago—

DUKE: What're you talkin' about?

JUDY: While you were over in Gollywood, hangin' around on some vine with your homeboy, Tarzan—

TRUCK: We been goin' crazy, man, lookin' for the surf! Everybody's goin' crazy.

JUDY: We looked all over. Duke. Surf's nowhere to be found—

TRUCK: Two weeks, not so much as a ripple! Check it out, man. Smooth as glass.

(They come to the edge of the stage and check it out.)

DUKE: You're right. I never seen it so smooth.

TRUCK: Where's the wave action? You know? Ocean's always got wave action. What's an ocean without wave action?

JUDY: I'm tellin' you. It's gone.

DUKE: Wow. Well, maybe this is some wacky Waikiki thing, man. Too many tourists, or something. You know, for bein' the most isolated place on earth, Hawaii can get awful crowded—

JUDY: We thought of that. It's not just Waikiki. We've checked everywhere, all over Oahu—

DUKE: North Shore? Always monster surf on the North Shore—

TRUCK: Nothin'. Not a splash. I get bigger waves runnin' tapwater in a glass than what's happening now with the waves on the North Shore.

DUKE: This is serious.

TRUCK: We're telling you, man. I mean, at first, we thought it was definitely some freak of nature, or something.

JUDY: No guestion—

TRUCK: But now—

JUDY: We think somebody stole it.

DUKE: Stole it?

JUDY: Stole it. Some guy.

TRUCK: How do you know it was a guy?

JUDY: It was definitely a guy. Girls don't do stupid stuff like that,

TRUCK: Oh, right.

JUDY: They don't.

TRUCK: I'm sure.

DUKE: What makes you think somebody stole the surf?

JUDY: I don't know. I just got a bad feeling about this—

DUKE: Nah. Gotta be a scientific explanation. Asteroids, or something. Meteor showers. Sun spots.

TRUCK: U F Os—

JUDY: U F Os aren't scientific. What a dweeb.

TRUCK: Shut up.

JUDY: Duke, how do we find out what's goin' on?

DUKE: We start lookin', that's how.

JUDY: Shouldn't we call the F B I or somethin'?

TRUCK: Oh, that's a good idea.

JUDY: Shut up.

DUKE: I'm the Sheriff of Honolulu—

JUDY: Hey, wow, check out the badge—

TRUCK: Cool—

DUKE: —and it's up to me to find out what's happened to Hawaii's surf. Forget the F B I. What do they know? Let's book!!

(*Travelling music. Lights change. They travel.* DUKE *comes downstage and talks to the audience.*)

DUKE: Man, they were right. There was no surf anywhere to be found. We did a quick circumnavigation around the entire island of Oahu—

(*The three of them walk in a big circle.*)

DUKE: —stopping to ask people if they'd seen any sign of surf in the last two weeks—

FIRST PERSON: Nope.

SECOND PERSON: Nope.

THIRD PERSON: Not hardly.

SECOND PERSON: Don't think so.

FIRST PERSON: No.

SECOND PERSON: Now that I think about it—no.

TRUCK: Duke, this is weird.

JUDY: Downright spooky.

DUKE: We did a quick canoe hop to the other Islands—

(They canoe hop to each island, DUKE *paddling like a champ,* JUDY *and* TRUCK *paddling for dear life—)*

DUKE: Did I mention I was a champion canoer?

TRUCK: *(Tongue hanging out)* No brag, no brag—

JUDY: *(Gasping for breath)* Just fact—where they're greeted with a shake of the head.

FIRST PERSON: Big Island, nope.

SECOND PERSON: Maui, nope.

THIRD PERSON: Molokai, no way.

FIRST PERSON: Lanai, forget about it.

SECOND PERSON: Kauai, I don't think so.

DUKE: No question about it. All over Hawaii, the surf was missing in action. And people were plenty upset.

(Crowd of three grumbles, then disappears.)

DUKE: When we got back to Honolulu, Truck and Judy were completely beat from all that canoe hopping around.

JUDY *and* TRUCK collapse.)

TRUCK: Man, I'm toast.

JUDY: Me, too. My arms are killing me.

TRUCK: Couch potato.

JUDY: Shut up.

DUKE: You kids. You're so outa shape. I barely broke a sweat.

(A piece of paper flutters down from the grid.)

DUKE: What's that?

TRUCK: Fanmail from some flounder?

JUDY: I'll get it.

(JUDY struggles to her feet, goes over and picks it up. It says "DUKE" on it in big letters.)

JUDY: Duke, it's for you.

DUKE: 'Course it's for me. This is my place. I'm the only person who gets mail here. Let me see it—

(JUDY ignores DUKE, opens the note, reads it. Her eyes get wide.)

DUKE: Judy, don't read my mail—

JUDY: It's a ransom note—

TRUCK: Wow! Cool!

DUKE: Ransom note? For what? What're you talking about?

(JUDY reads the note. Her eyes widen.)

JUDY: Holy smokes! *(Reads)* "Dear Mr Kahanamoku. Don't bother looking for the Hawaiian Surf. I've got it in a place where you'll never find it. I'll be in touch soon to tell you my demands. Don't call anyone — especially the F B I—

TRUCK: See? Told you—

JUDY: Shut up. *(Reads)* —if you ever want to see your precious Hawaiian surf again. Sincerely, The Surfnappers."

TRUCK: Sincerely, the Surfnappers?

JUDY: Really polite ransom note. Didn't even mention money.

DUKE: Maybe they don't want money.

JUDY: See? What'd I tell you? Some guy stole the surf—

TRUCK: Get off it. You don't know it's a guy. Could be a girl—

JUDY: No way.

TRUCK: Why'd they send the ransom note to you?

DUKE: You know a more famous Hawaiian?

TRUCK: Nope.

DUKE: The symbol of his people?

TRUCK: No question.

DUKE: The personification of the aloha spirit?

TRUCK: That's you.

DUKE: There you go. Who else would they send it to?

TRUCK: Nobody but you, Duke.

DUKE: Thank you.

JUDY: Think it's for real?

DUKE: Probably some kook, but I guess we'd better check it out. Let's book.

(*Travelling music. They book some more.*)

JUDY: Kook? I like you, Duke, you're way cool for an older guy, but isn't kook just a little—square?

DUKE: I like kook. Kook is cool.

JUDY: O-kay—

(*They get to the ocean. Peaceful ocean sounds. They look out. Their faces tell the story.*)

JUDY: Still missing.

DUKE: I never thought about what the ocean would look like without surf.

TRUCK: It looks awful. Smooth—

JUDY: It doesn't look like itself—

TRUCK: No wave action.

DUKE: Let's ask somebody if they've seen anything suspicious goin' down around here recently—

(A BIG GUY *comes onstage.)*

TRUCK: Hey, bra—

BIG GUY: Wha? Hey, Duke! Duke! Duke Kahanamoku! Howzit?

*(*DUKE *beams.* DUKE *and* BIG GUY *shake hands.)*

JUDY: *(To* TRUCK*)* He's so famous.

TRUCK: Really.

BIG GUY: Hey. Everybody know Duke.

DUKE: Listen, Big Guy. You seen anything suspicious goin' down around here recently?

BIG GUY: You mean, like, criminal activity?

DUKE: Possibly—

BIG GUY: Hey, Duke. Aren't you kinda outa your jurisdiction? Over here on the North Shore's a long way from Honolulu—

DUKE: Don't tell anybody, but—I'm on special assignment.

BIG GUY: Nah! Wha?

DUKE: You notice anything peculiar around here lately?

BIG GUY: Just the usual misdemeanors. Nothin' heavy—

DUKE: What about the ocean?

BIG GUY: Ocean?

DUKE: Notice anything strange about the ocean?

*(*BIG GUY *thinks it over, shakes his head.)*

BIG GUY: No.

(DUKE *gently turns* BIG GUY *around and faces him towards the ocean.*)

DUKE: There. Tell me what you see.

(BIG GUY *studies it hard for a minute.*)

BIG GUY: Water, eh?

DUKE: What about the water?

BIG GUY: Blue, eh?

DUKE: What else?

BIG GUY: Big, eh?

DUKE: What else?

BIG GUY: Wet, eh?

(DUKE *sighs, pats* BIG GUY *on the shoulder.*)

DUKE: Okay, Big Guy. Thanks for your help.

(DUKE *and* BIG GUY *shake hands.*)

BIG GUY: Anytime, Duke. Anything I can do to help you out, let me know—

DUKE: We'll be in touch.

BIG GUY: Okay. *(He exits.)*

TRUCK: Wow. He didn't even notice the surf is missing. Scary.

JUDY: Makes you realize how many people would never even know the surf was gone if it disappeared for good. Which it's not gonna do.

TRUCK: No way.

DUKE: Not gonna happen.

JUDY: So, Duke. What do we do now?

(*An* OLD LADY *enters.*)

DUKE: Let's ask this nice Old Lady if she's seen anything supicious goin' down around here—

OLD LADY: I'm so glad you asked me that question.

DUKE: I haven't asked you yet.

OLD LADY: I heard you, I heard you. I may be old, but I'm not deaf.

JUDY: Hearing impaired.

OLD LADY: Excuse me?

JUDY: You're supposed to say hearing impaired. Not deaf. Deaf's not nice.

OLD LADY: Don't tell me what to say, kid. I'm too old to be bossed around.

JUDY: Chronologically gifted.

OLD LADY: Excuse me?

JUDY: You're supposed to say chronologically gifted, not old. Old's not nice—

OLD LADY: I'm sorry, I can't hear you, I'm going deaf because I'm so old. Now clam up before I have to clock you one.

(TRUCK *smirks at* JUDY.)

JUDY: Shut up.

OLD LADY: I believe the question was, have I seen anything suspicious?

DUKE: Yes, ma'am.

OLD LADY: Well, for starters—

(OLD LADY *drags* DUKE *over to look at the ocean.*)

OLD LADY: Take a look at that ocean. Tell me what you see.

DUKE: I see an ocean with no surf.

OLD LADY: Darn tootin' you do! At last! Somebody with eyes in his head instead of marbles! (*Notices badge*) You some kinda lawman?

DUKE: I'm the Sheriff of Honolulu. Duke Kahanamoku. Maybe you've heard of me?

OLD LADY: Nope.

TRUCK: *(to* JUDY*)* Not that famous.

JUDY: Shut up.

OLD LADY: What're ya doin' all the way over here?

DUKE: Investigating the missing surf.

OLD LADY: I've been waitin' for somebody with the good sense God gave 'em to come around and ask me about this very subject. I know who took the surf.

DUKE: You do?

OLD LADY: I do.

DUKE: Who?

OLD LADY: Some guy—

JUDY: See? Told you—

TRUCK: Shut up.

OLD LADY: He was down there on the beach for weeks, measuring and calculatin'. I wondered what he was up to. Figured he was just another developer, gonna put up another five-star resort. So I started comin' down here at night, to appreciate the beach before it disappeared, because once those five-star resorts go up—you know what I'm sayin', young fella?

DUKE: Yes, ma'am.

OLD LADY: So one night, I'm down here, takin' in the full moon on the water—

(Music cue: flashback suspense music. MR DOUBLE BOGEY, *dressed in a white suit, panama hat, a stuffed green parrot on one shoulder, walks with a limp, and carries a golf club, and his assistant,* ARMOND, *who has lots of tattoos, enter.)*

OLD LADY: —and there's this same guy standin' on the beach. And he's got a creepy buddy with him. And they look around to see if anybody's watchin'—

(They look around.)

OLD LADY: —and then they pull this weird lookin' contraption out of its case, looked kinda like a ray gun—

(They come up with a weird contraption.)

OLD LADY: And they point it at the surf—

(They do.)

OLD LADY: —which is all silver and white in the moonlight—and they pull the trigger—

(They pull the trigger.)

OLD LADY: —and this green electricity crackles out—

(It does.)

OLD LADY: —and the surf goes electric psychedelic green. And then they flick a switch and throw this ray gun or whatever into reverse—

(They do.)

OLD LADY: —and it sucks up all the surf, and leaves the water smooth as a baby's you-know-what.

DUKE: Wow.

OLD LADY: Wow is right, young fella.

DUKE: Then what happened?

OLD LADY: Then they booked.

(MR DOUBLE BOGEY and ARMOND book on out.)

TRUCK: Surfnapping.

DUKE: They musta just driven up the beach to the next batch of surf.

JUDY: Yeah. They coulda done the whole island in one night.

TRUCK: Easy.

DUKE: Think you'd recognize this guy if you saw him again?

OLD LADY: I don't know. My eyesight's not so good. I'm half-blind. *(To* JUDY*)* Don't start with me, kid. You say visually challenged, and you're history—

DUKE: What do you remember about him? Anything special? Any distinguishing characteristics?

OLD LADY: Pretty average. Nothin' to write home about.

DUKE: Anything. Anything unusual at all.

OLD LADY: Not really. Except for the limp.

DUKE: Limp.

OLD LADY: And the patch over one eye.

DUKE: Patch.

OLD LADY: But that's pretty common. And that white suit he's wears all the time—

DUKE: White suit?

OLD LADY: And the green parrot on his shoulder. Dime a dozen.

JUDY: Parrots.

TRUCK: Parrots are out, man.

JUDY: Parrots are passe. Totally. Everybody's doin' 'em.

OLD LADY: Not even a live parrot. This particular parrot is dead. Stuffed.

JUDY: Good idea. Less mess.

TRUCK: Yeah. I mean, with a white suit, you don't want a real parrot on your shoulder—

DUKE: Limp, patch, white suit, stuffed parrot. Not much to go on. Anything else?

OLD LADY: Always carries a golf club. Like I said. Perfectly normal fella. Unremarkable. Nope. I'm afraid you're gonna have a hard time finding this guy. Joe Average.

DUKE: Well, we'll do our best. What about his sidekick?

OLD LADY: Nothing unusual about him, either. Nothing at all. Getting all those tattoos must've hurt, though.

DUKE: Well. Thank you for your co-operation, ma'am.

OLD LADY: Good luck. (*She starts out. Turns back*) What'd you say your name was?

DUKE: Duke Kahanamoku.

OLD LADY: You wouldn't be related to Sergeant Kahanamoku, would you?

DUKE: Yes, ma'am. He's my brother.

OLD LADY: Now there's a good looking guy.

(OLD LADY *exits.* TRUCK *and* JUDY *smirk at* DUKE.)

DUKE: Shut up. Let's go find this guy—

Travelling music. DUKE exits. JUDY and TRUCK follow.

JUDY: I told you it was a guy—

TRUCK: Shut up.

(*They exit, too.* ARMOND *pushes on an aquarium, which is filled with surging surf, followed onstage by* MR DOUBLE BOGEY.)

ARMOND: Boss. Tell me again why we stole the surf.

MR DOUBLE BOGEY: We're gonna make a deal.

ARMOND: What kinda deal?

MR DOUBLE BOGEY: A very big kind of deal. What other kind of deal is there?

ARMOND: So, are we gonna give the surf back, or what?

MR DOUBLE BOGEY: Maybe. If we can make this deal. Otherwise, we'll dump it somewhere.

ARMOND: I hope we can make this deal. 'Cause I'd like to go surfing. I ain't been surfing since we stole the surf, and I miss it.

MR DOUBLE BOGEY: If you miss surfing so much, there's always Australia—

ARMOND: Boss. Please.

MR DOUBLE BOGEY: Don't worry. We'll make this deal.

ARMOND: But what are you gonna do with all this surf?

MR DOUBLE BOGEY: I'm gonna swap it.

ARMOND: For what?

MR DOUBLE BOGEY: For Hawaii.

ARMOND: For Hawaii?

MR DOUBLE BOGEY: You heard me. For Hawaii.

ARMOND: You mean—the Big Island?

MR DOUBLE BOGEY: I mean, all of it.

ARMOND: All of it?

MR DOUBLE BOGEY: Will you quit repeating everything I say? I already have one parrot. And, in case you hadn't noticed, he's dead. And stuffed. Get the picture?

ARMOND: Yes, boss. You were saying?

MR DOUBLE BOGEY: I'm going to make a deal to swap the surf back to Hawaii, in exchange for—

ARMOND: Hawaii.

MR DOUBLE BOGEY: Precisely.

ARMOND: All of it.

MR DOUBLE BOGEY: Most of it. I don't need the really steep parts. They can keep the upper slopes of the volcanoes.

ARMOND: And what are you gonna do with Hawaii?

(MR DOUBLE BOGEY *takes a swing with his golf club and smiles a really evil smile.*)

MR DOUBLE BOGEY: I'm gonna turn the Hawaiian Islands into the world's biggest golf course slash convention center.

ARMOND: *(Shrugs)* Okay with me. As long as there's surfing.

MR DOUBLE BOGEY: Precisely. That's how most people feel. As long as they have their own little personal amusements, they won't care that I've turned the islands into one big sand trap and water hazard. We'll put up some Nintendo arcades for the kids—and everyone will be happy.

ARMOND: Everyone?

MR DOUBLE BOGEY: There're always a few malcontents moping about. That's why we have to make this deal with Duke Kahanamoku. He can bring the hotheads on board.

ARMOND: Think he'll go for it?

MR DOUBLE BOGEY: Oh, yeah. He loves surfing just about as much as I love golf. (*He takes a swing, and laughs his evil laugh.*)

ARMOND: Wish they'd hurry up and get here. I need to get out on my boogie board and curl some slappers.

MR DOUBLE BOGEY: Whatever that means.

(MR DOUBLE BOGEY *walks out.* ARMOND *follows.*)

ARMOND: You should try surfing sometime, boss. It's bitchin'.

MR DOUBLE BOGEY: No thanks. I don't like to mess up my hair. Nintendo, surfing, waterslides, hang gliding, jet skis, helicopter rides, dirt bikes, submarines—we'll have it all—

(MR DOUBLE BOGEY and ARMOND are gone. Music. DUKE, JUDY and TRUCK enter.)

JUDY: You'd think those guys wouldn't be that hard to find. I mean, it's like not that huge of an island—

DUKE: Shhh. What's that?

(They listen.)

TRUCK: I know that sound.

JUDY: So do I

DUKE: It's surf!

(They whirl around and see the surf aquarium.)

JUDY: Wow. A box of surf.

TRUCK: Looks like somebody put a blender in an aquarium.

DUKE: Hmmm. This could be a clue.

MR DOUBLE BOGEY: *(Offstage)* Possibly.

(DUKE, JUDY and TRUCK whirl around to see MR DOUBLE BOGEY and ARMOND standing there. DUKE checks them out.)

DUKE: White suit, stuffed parrot, patch, limp, tattoos. I think you guys are just the guys we're looking for.

MR DOUBLE BOGEY: Very perceptive. Sheriff Kahanamoku, I presume.

JUDY: *(To TRUCK)* Guy's a rock star, I'm telling you. Even the bad guys know him—

TRUCK: I'm impressed.

JUDY: Notice I said bad guys—

TRUCK: Shut up.

MR DOUBLE BOGEY: Allow me to introduce myself. I am Mr Double Bogey—

DUKE: Mr Double Bogey, huh?

MR DOUBLE BOGEY: Heard of me?

DUKE: No.

MR DOUBLE BOGEY: Oh. Well. I'm sure we'll become very close personal friends.

JUDY: Not.

MR DOUBLE BOGEY: And this is my faithful companion, Armond.

JUDY: Cool tattoos, dude.

ARMOND: Thanks.

TRUCK: Did it hurt?

ARMOND: A lot.

JUDY: I'll bet. I mean, look at this

guy. Duke. This guy is totally sleeved—

DUKE: Very nice. So, Mr Double Bogey. What'd you do with the surf?

MR DOUBLE BOGEY: What surf?

DUKE: Don't play dumb with me. The surf you swiped from Hawaii. Where is it?

JUDY: Yeah. Cough it up, surfnapper.

TRUCK: Yeah. Give it back right now or we're gonna have to get tough—

MR DOUBLE BOGEY: Oh, I wouldn't, if I were you.

DUKE: Or what?

MR DOUBLE BOGEY: Or you'll never see your precious surf again. It'll be gone forever, like one of those rare species of Hawaiian songbird that is now extinct.

ARMOND: He means it. Better do what he says. Please. Or we'll all be hangin' ten Down Under—

DUKE: Alright. What's the deal?

MR DOUBLE BOGEY: A simple swap. I give Hawaii back its surf—

DUKE: Yeah?

MR DOUBLE BOGEY: And you give me — Hawaii.

ARMOND: That's fair. Really.

JUDY: Let me get this straight. You want the whole Big Island? Are you nuts?

MR DOUBLE BOGEY: Not just the Big Island. All the Islands.

JUDY: All of all the Islands?

MR DOUBLE BOGEY: Just the good parts. You can keep the steep places where you have to stand kinda at a forty-five degree angle.

JUDY: What're you gonna do with all of the Hawaiian Islands?

MR DOUBLE BOGEY: I need 'em for a golf course.

DUKE: A golf course.

MR DOUBLE BOGEY: And convention center.

DUKE: That's a good way to use 'em.

MR DOUBLE BOGEY: It'll be spectacular. World's biggest. Something every Hawaiian can be proud of.

DUKE: I don't think so.

MR DOUBLE BOGEY: Don't be too hasty. Sheriff.

DUKE: How do we know you've even got the surf?

(MR DOUBLE BOGEY *gestures to the aquarium.*)

MR DOUBLE BOGEY: There's a sample. Smell it. Taste it. Listen to it. Go ahead. Stick your face in it.

(DUKE *goes over to the aquarium, sticks his head in. Smells it, tastes it, listens to it.*)

MR DOUBLE BOGEY: Well?

DUKE: That's Waikiki surf, all right. No question. Where's the rest of it?

MR DOUBLE BOGEY: In a very very very safe place.

TRUCK: Must be a very large very safe place. That's a lotta surf you're napping, pal.

MR DOUBLE BOGEY: I have unlimited storage facilities, believe me. Well? Do we have a deal or what?

DUKE: I don't know. I have to think about it.

MR DOUBLE BOGEY: What's to think about? I know you can't live without your precious surf, Sheriff. Come on. You'll never even notice. You'll be too busy surfing. What's the difference, one more golf course?

(DUKE *considers.* JUDY *and* TRUCK *eye him anxiously.* DUKE *sighs deeply.*)

DUKE: Okay. You got a deal.

(JUDY *and* TRUCK *are aghast.*)

TRUCK: What??!?

JUDY: Duke!!?!

TRUCK: What're you doing, man?

(MR DOUBLE BOGEY *smiles his evil smile.*)

MR DOUBLE BOGEY: Excellent. Meet me here in twenty-four hours, and we'll swap. If you're not here, you can kiss your precious surf adieu, adios, aloha, sayonara, say goodnight Gracie. I'll destroy it, mess it up, do a number on it, permanently, irrevocably, no refunds, no exchanges, tough luck, and you'll never get it back. Do I make myself clear?

DUKE: You're like the mongoose. You're supposed to do something good for the Islands, and instead you fix something that wasn't broke, wreck it forever, and call it progress.

MR DOUBLE BOGEY: Actually I call it eighteen holes of Heaven, and a challenging par. And I don't care if you call me a mongoose, I like mongooses. They're furry, and they're cuddly, and they're cute. But enough name calling. Do we have a deal?

DUKE: We'll be here.

JUDY: Speak for yourself—

(JUDY *starts to storm out, but* DUKE *grabs her.*)

MR DOUBLE BOGEY: See you then. And remember. Not a word of this to anyone. Especially the F B I—

JUDY: Shut up.

MR DOUBLE BOGEY: *(To* JUDY*)* I like you. You'd make a great caddy. And you could be attractive, if you'd just get rid of that baseball cap and put on a dress—

JUDY: Why, I oughta—Duke! Let me at him! Let me go!

(MR DOUBLE BOGEY *and* ARMOND *exit.* DUKE *lets* JUDY *go.*)

JUDY: Duke! How could you? Make a deal like that? Sell out Hawaii—

TRUCK: Shut up.

JUDY: What? Are you on his side? Truck, I thought you were my pal. Just 'cause you wanna surf! That's no reason to sell out Hawaii! Heck, I wanna surf, too—

TRUCK: He didn't sell out Hawaii. Didja, Duke?

DUKE: Nope.

TRUCK: He's just playin' for time. Right?

DUKE: Right.

TRUCK: So cool your jets.

JUDY: Oh. Okay. Sure. I knew that. Alla time.

DUKE: Besides, how could I make a deal like that?
Hawaii's not mine to sell out. Twenty-four hours. We
got exactly twenty-four hours to find the surf, destroy
Mr. Double Bogey's surfnapping device, and get the
surf back where it belongs.

JUDY: Don't forget put Mr Double Bogey's double-
crossing butt in jail.

DUKE: That, too.

TRUCK: So where would those crooks hide Hawaii's
surf?

JUDY: Got to be a really monstrous big place.

DUKE: Where's a place big enough in the Islands to
hide all that surf?

(They ponder this for a moment. DUKE snaps his fingers.)

DUKE: I got it. Let's book!

(Travelling music. They book. They get to the shore.)

JUDY: We goin' to the Big Island?

DUKE: Yup. Wanna swim or canoe?

TRUCK: We didn't bring our paddles.

DUKE: Dive in.

*(DUKE dives in, followed by JUDY and TRUCK. DUKE swims
like a champ, of course, while TRUCK and JUDY swim for
dear life.)*

JUDY: *(Gasping for breath)* Isn't he a gold medal winner?

TRUCK: *(Gasping for breath)* Yeah—double—gold—

*(They get to the shore of the Big Island. JUDY and TRUCK
flop.)*

JUDY: I'm toast.

TRUCK: I'm history.

DUKE: Don't fade now. We got a ways to go. Let's book.

(DUKE *books on out of there.* JUDY *and* TRUCK *groan, get up and book out after* DUKE. DUKE *reappears. Followed by an exhausted* TRUCK *and* JUDY. *They join* DUKE, *who is looking down into: The crater of the volcano. Red light and steam.*)

JUDY: Wow. The crater of the volcano.

TRUCK: Kilauea.

JUDY: It's humongous.

TRUCK: The perfect hiding spot for Hawaii's surf.

DUKE: Except for one thing.

TRUCK: It's too hot!

JUDY: There's no surf—

DUKE: Just red-hot molten magma—

JUDY: And a little salt-water steam—

TRUCK: Oh, no! It's evaporated!

JUDY: Totally!

TRUCK: That idiot Mr Double Bogey destroyed the surf after all!

JUDY: What a bozo!

TRUCK: What a mongoose!

JUDY: What a wombat!

TRUCK: What a dweeb!

DUKE: I guess that's it, then.

JUDY: No more surf in Hawaii.

TRUCK: Mr Double Bogey'll probably go ahead and turn the Islands into a golf course, anyway.

JUDY: Yeah, probably.

DUKE: Not if I can help it.

JUDY: Me, too.

TRUCK: Me, too.

DUKE: I am gonna miss surfing, though.

JUDY: Me, too.

TRUCK: Me, too.

(They stare glumly into the crater.)

TRUCK: There's always Australia.

JUDY: Not.

DUKE: Uh huh.

JUDY: Don't think so.

DUKE: No way.

JUDY: Never.

DUKE: Look under "fat chance".

JUDY: Look under "I'd rather die".

TRUCK: Okay, okay.

(PRINCESS PELE appears out of the volcano. She's a modern volcano princess, chewing gum, wearing the latest.)

PRINCESS PELE: Hi!

DUKE: Oh, my goodness—it's Pele!

PRINCESS PELE: No. That's my mom. I'm Princess Pele. You guys looking for the surf?

DUKE: Yeah. We were, but—

PRINCESS PELE: Yeah. You know, those bad guys were really really stupid.

JUDY: Tell us about it.

PRINCESS PELE: I mean, everybody knows when you dump a bunch of water into a volcano, it's gonna evaporate. We couldn't believe it. My mom was really mad. She thought they were trying to, like, put our fire out. Douse our lava. I mean, like, no way. No way that could ever happen. Dream on.

DUKE: So what happened?

PRINCESS PELE: Oh, she saved most of the surf, before it could evaporate.

(DUKE, JUDY *and* TRUCK *cheer.*)

JUDY: Yea!

TRUCK: Cool!

DUKE: Right on! So where is it?

PRINCESS PELE: My mom has it.

JUDY: Fantastic!

TRUCK: Way cool!

PRINCESS PELE: You're Duke Kahanamoku, right?

JUDY: *(To* TRUCK*)* He's a superstar, I'm telling you. Even the volcano goddesses know who he is.

TRUCK: I'm impressed, I'm impressed.

PRINCESS PELE: Oh, sure, we know Duke Kahanamoku. We follow sports. *(To* DUKE*)* Love your shirt.

DUKE: Thanks. So your mom—has the surf?

PRINCESS PELE: Yeah.

DUKE: Can we get it back?

PRINCESS PELE: Maybe.

DUKE: Great. Show us where it is, and we'll take it back. I mean, we didn't bring any containers with us, but we'll figure out something. Maybe you could lend us a hand—

PRINCESS PELE: There's just one thing.

DUKE: What's that?

PRINCESS PELE: My mom, she's been real upset, the last hundred years or so, with what's been going on in the Islands and all—

DUKE: Right—

JUDY: We can relate to that—

PRINCESS PELE: And before she gives the surf back to the people of Hawaii, she wants to make sure they appreciate what they've got—

TRUCK: Oh, we do, we do. I mean, we could be in Australia, for instance. Think about it!

PRINCESS PELE: That's not enough. Like, just bein' grateful you're in Hawaii instead of Australia or Cleveland isn't nearly enough. That's easy. I mean, like, who wouldn't be. No. She wants to make sure the people love Hawaii and know what they've got here — wait, she gave me a list— *(Pulls out list, reads)* "How precious, how beautiful, how unigue, how totally irreplaceable Hawaii is"—

DUKE: I know all that stuff.

JUDY: Me, too. We love Hawaii!

TRUCK: We do!

DUKE: But how do we prove that to her?

PRINCESS PELE: She has a small task for you.

DUKE: Name it.

(PRINCESS PELE consults her mom's note.)

PRINCESS PELE: *(Reads)* "The surf is gone. Find the surf."

JUDY: What does that mean?

PRINCESS PELE: Hey, that's my mom. I mean, I love her to death, but sometimes she's a little obscure. Hey, she's a volcano goddess, she can be as obscure as she wants to be.

DUKE: The surf is gone. Find the surf. Okay.

PRINCESS PELE: Good luck. *(She exits.)*

JUDY: Now what do we do?

DUKE: We find the surf.

TRUCK: But the surf's gone—

DUKE: Let's island hop.

(Hopping music. They hop. They paddle. They swim. From island to island. They stop. They're exhausted. Discouraged)

JUDY: There's no surf. Anywhere.

TRUCK: I'm toast. *(He collapses.)*

JUDY: Couch potato.

TRUCK: Shut up.

DUKE: I got an idea. Let's book. Let's book where we've never booked before.

TRUCK: Can we fly there? I'm really tired.

DUKE: You kids are so outa shape. Come on.

(Travelling music. DUKE pulls JUDY and TRUCK to their feet. They book, DUKE dragging them. They stop. They look around.)

JUDY: Wow. Where are we?

TRUCK: I never been here before.

JUDY: I've been everywhere in the Islands.

DUKE: Niihau.

JUDY: Niihau!

TRUCK: Niihau!

DUKE: Look out there. What do you see?

(They go to the edge of the stage. The sound of surf)

JUDY: Surf!

TRUCK: Surf!

DUKE: You got it.

JUDY: Okay, so tell us.

TRUCK: Don't keep us in suspense.

JUDY: Why's there surf here on Niihau and nowhere else?

(MR DOUBLE BOGEY *and* ARMOND *enter, surfnapping device in hand, sneak up on our heroes.* ARMOND *slips a big plastic inner tube over* TRUCK *and* JUDY, *immobilizing them.*)

MR DOUBLE BOGEY: Because we haven't gotten here yet. Just give me a second, and I'll make Niihau like everywhere else.

DUKE: You can't make Niihau part of your golfcourse—

MR DOUBLE BOGEY: Oh, yeah? Who's gonna stop me? And don't try to rescue your friends, or I'll hit—

(*Suspense music cue*)

MR DOUBLE BOGEY: The evaporate button!

ARMOND: Oh, boss! Not the evaporate button!

MR DOUBLE BOGEY: Then don't make me angry. Stand back! I'm gonna add Niihau to our collection— (*He points his surfnapping device at the Niihau surf.*) BOGEY: Watch this—

(MR DOUBLE BOGEY *fires the surfnapping device at the Niihau surf. The green electricity crackles, but—*)

JUDY: Nothing happened!

TRUCK: Yea! Hooray!

JUDY: Take that, you wombat!

MR DOUBLE BOGEY: Shut up. I don't understand! I don't know what went wrong. I've still got the warranty on this thing—

DUKE: Because the people of Niihau have kept faith with the old ways. And the old spirit of aloha. And old Hawaii. So your surfnapping device had no effect on this Niihau surf—

(OLD LADY OF NIIHAU enters.)

OLD LADY: Hey, bad guys—

MR DOUBLE BOGEY: Wha?

OLD LADY: You have tried to steal the surf of Niihau with your ray gun—

MR DOUBLE BOGEY: Hey. It was an honest mistake.

OLD LADY: So we curse you—

ARMOND: You shouldn't curse, a nice old lady like you—

OLD LADY: With Pele's curse—

(The OLD LADY OF NIIHAU exits, smiling. DUKE, JUDY, and TRUCK look at each other.)

TRUCK: Pele's curse?

JUDY: Uh oh.

TRUCK: You guys are toast. Literally.

MR DOUBLE BOGEY: *(To ARMOND)* We better book.

ARMOND: Fast forward, dude.

MR DOUBLE BOGEY: *(To DUKE)* We still have a deal. You can keep Niihau, but bring the deed to the rest of the Islands tomorrow. Or else. I hit the evaporate button on Hawaii's surf— *(To ARMOND, re: JUDY and TRUCK)* Throw those two to the sharks.

ARMOND: Why?

MR DOUBLE BOGEY: For practice.

ARMOND: Okay—

(ARMOND *picks up* JUDY *and* TRUCK, *still immobilized
by the inner tube, and throws them over the cliff. There's a
long whistling sound as they descend, followed by a beat of
silence, then the sound of a large splash, and a wave of water
splashes onstage. From far away, tiny little voices cry:*)

JUDY: *(Offstage)* Help! Duke! Help!

TRUCK: *(Offstage)* Help! Duke! Help!

DUKE: You'll get yours.

MR DOUBLE BOGEY: I certainly intend to. Armond?
Let's boogie—

(ARMOND *and* MR DOUBLE BOGEY *boogie out.* JUDY *and*
TRUCK *are still crying for help.*)

(DUKE *dives off the cliff. A whistling sound, a silence, a
splash, a wave of water. A* SHARK *swims by, in the general
direction of our heroes. Offstage,* TRUCK *and* JUDY *scream.
The sound of the* SHARK *being bopped on the nose.* SHARK
*reappears, whimpering like a kicked dog, and disappears from
whence it came. Moments later, all three of them emerge,
soaking wet.*)

TRUCK: Thanks, Duke.

JUDY: Yeah, thanks. You bopped that one shark on the
snout pretty good. Where'd you learn to do that?

DUKE: Seemed like the thing to do. Much as I hate to
say it, we'd better go see what's happened to those
guys. They don't know what they're in for, with Pele's
curse.

TRUCK: Yeah. We better hurry.

JUDY: Not.

(*They laugh and book out in slow motion. The red light and
steam of Kilauea appear.* ARMOND *and* MR DOUBLE BOGEY
enter, with their surfnapping device.)

MR DOUBLE BOGEY: Time to check on our precious commodity.

ARMOND: You really gonna give the surf back, boss?

MR DOUBLE BOGEY: Are you crazy? What self-respecting villain would ever live up to his end of a deal? No way. I'm gonna corner the market on Hawaiian surf. I'll export it all over the world. I'll franchise it.

ARMOND: Franchise it!

MR DOUBLE BOGEY: You bet! I call it—McSurf!

ARMOND: McSurf. I'm there. *(He goes to the edge of the crater and looks in.)*

ARMOND: Uh, boss—

MR DOUBLE BOGEY: What's the problem?

ARMOND: Where's our surf?

MR DOUBLE BOGEY: Don't be ridiculous— *(He goes to the edge and looks in.)* Why, this is outrageous! Some thief has stolen our surf! Armond! Call 911!

ARMOND: Okay, boss—

(But before ARMOND *and* MR DOUBLE BOGEY *can move, there's an ominous rumble.)*

MR DOUBLE BOGEY: What's that?

*(*ARMOND *and* MR DOUBLE BOGEY *start to shake 'n bake.)*

ARMOND: Uh oh! Shake 'n bake!

MR DOUBLE BOGEY: Run for the border!

ARMOND: Boss, there is no border, we're on an island!

MR DOUBLE BOGEY: Right. I forgot.

(A large mass of red gooey lava falls on them from the sky and smothers them. Music. DUKE, TRUCK *and* JUDY *enter.* DUKE *has a box of Niihau surf. They see the lava lump.)*

JUDY: Oops.

TRUCK: Guess we shoulda booked a little harder.

JUDY: Shouldna stopped for that shave ice in Hilo—

DUKE: Look around, see if you can find their surfnapping device.

(TRUCK *finds it, picks it up.*)

TRUCK: Here it is. *(To audience)* This is not a toy.

DUKE: Let's test it.

(DUKE *puts the box of Niihau surf down.* TRUCK *aims the surfnapper at it:*)

DUKE: Let 'er rip!

(TRUCK *fires the surfnapper. It crackles with green electricity, but nothing happens to the surf.*)

DUKE: See?

JUDY: Niihau surf—

TRUCK: Way cool.

(PRINCESS PELE *enters.*)

PRINCESS PELE: I see you found the surf.

DUKE: I hope your mother's pleased.

PRINCESS PELE: Not quite yet—but she's getting there. She wants Duke Kahanamoku to deliver the surf back to all the people of Hawaii personally.

DUKE: How do I do that?

PRINCESS PELE: By surfing, of course. The surf will follow everywhere you go. Try it.

(PRINCESS PELE *exits.* DUKE *looks at* JUDY *and* TRUCK. *They groan.*)

DUKE: Come on. It'll go faster if we all pitch in.

JUDY: Okay—

TRUCK: Okay—

DUKE: For this we need a real board. An old board. A royal koa board.

(JUDY *and* TRUCK *follow up to the big statue board, and hop on.*)

DUKE: Let's go.

(*Music. They surf all around all the Islands. They finish. They hop off.* PRINCESS PELE *reappears.*)

JUDY: Aren't we done yet?

PRINCESS PELE: One more thing. Say the prayer.

JUDY: Totally.

TRUCK: Let's do it. Duke?

(DUKE *holds up the box of Niihau surf. The four of them dip their hands in the water, then flick their fingers towards the audience, gently blessing them with drops of water, while reciting a short prayer in Hawaiian, celebrating the surf. They finish. A cloud of steam rises from Kilauea.*)

PRINCESS PELE: My mother says— (*She translates the steam.*) When you get back to Waikiki, have a thousand-yard ride for her.

(DUKE, JUDY *and* TRUCK *cheer. The trio slaps five all around.* PRINCESS PELE *exits.*)

JUDY: Cool.

TRUCK: Way cool.

DUKE: Hey, guys. Mahalo.

TRUCK: Anytime.

JUDY: See you back at wacky Waikiki.

DUKE: Aloha.

(JUDY *and* TRUCK *exit.* DUKE *addresses the audience.*)

DUKE: When I first broke the world record for the hundred meters, nobody believed me. They didn't believe that a Waikiki beach boy with a funny name like me could do such a thing. So they disallowed it. I didn't care. I knew I had broken the record. After all, I was there. Besides, after I won the Gold medal, then they believed me. *(He hops back up on the pedestal—)* So that's the story of how I saved the surf for Hawaii. See? When you put your mind to it, you can do anything. Even save Hawaii.

(Music: Gabby Pahanui)

DUKE: Hey, there's my pal Gabby again. Beautiful music, isn't it?

(Lights up on Gabby screen.)

DUKE: You know. Gabby had to work all his life at another job. Road crew for the county. He worked hard. He could never make a living just playing music. But it was what he loved, and he never gave up on it. And that's the thing you have to remember. Never give up on the thing you love to do. Like surfing. Or playing music. If you never give up on it, it'll never give up on you. And that what art is. And that's what will make you an artist. Whether you're surfing or playing music or dancing hula or whatever. Anyway, where was I? Oh, yeah.

(—and becomes the statue again. Music. After a moment, the teen-age BOY *and* GIRL *from the Prologue enter.)*

BOY: Hey, here's that statue again.

GIRL: I found out who he is.

BOY: Who?

GIRL: Duke Kahanamoku.

BOY: Who's he?

GIRL: He was a famous swimmer. He won gold medals. He practically invented surfing. He made Hawaiian shirts popular, and Hawaiian music, he was really famous, he was even the Sheriff of Honolulu.

BOY: Wow. That's fantastic.

GIRL: Yeah. And when Duke died, it was real stormy the day of his funeral, and they took a bunch of outrigger canoes and paddled out through the surf at Waikiki to scatter his ashes over the ocean, and at that moment the sun came out and there were rainbows all over the place.

BOY: Wow. A real hero.

GIRL: Yeah.

BOY: Like, if he was such a famous surfer and swimmer and canoer and stuff—shouldn't his statue be facing the ocean?

GIRL: Somebody messed up. As usual.

(BOY *shrugs, looks at* GIRL. *They go over to the statue, and turn it around so it faces the ocean.*)

BOY: There. That's better. That's the way it's supposed to be.

GIRL: That wasn't so hard.

BOY: Nope.

GIRL: If you put your mind to it, you can do anything.

BOY: Yup. Let's put our mind to a pizza. Whaddya say?

GIRL: Totally. I'm there.

(*Music.* BOY *and* GIRL *exit. Lights hit each of the hero Dukes in turn: Duke Snyder, Duke Ellington. The lights fade until there's a light only on Duke Kahanamoku. The last light fades out.*)

END OF PLAY

www.ingramcontent.com/pod-product-compliance
Lightning Source LLC
Chambersburg PA
CBHW060526110426
42741CB00042B/2776